CARNIVAL

CARNIVAL

A CELEBRATION OF WARWICKSHIRE POETRY

Compiled and Edited by
DAVID HOWE

WARWICKSHIRE BOOKS

WEST MIDLANDS ARTS
FUNDED

First published in Great Britain in 1989 by Warwickshire Books

British Library Cataloguing-in-Publication Data
Carnival: a celebration of Warwickshire poetry.
1. Poetry in English. School Student writers, 1945–
Anthologies
821'.914'08099282

ISBN 1–871942–00–4

Printed and Bound in Great Britain by BPCC Wheatons Ltd

WARWICKSHIRE BOOKS

Official Publisher to Warwickshire County Council

An imprint of Wheaton Publishers Ltd. A Member of Maxwell Pergamon Publishing Corporation plc

Wheaton Publishers Ltd
Hennock Road, Marsh Barton, Exeter, Devon EX2 8RP
Tel: 0392 74121; Telex 42794 (WHEATN G)

SALES

Direct sales enquiries to Warwickshire Books at the address above.

Illustrations by Mark Hannon

The Warwickshire Poetry Carnival (1988–9)

THE IDEA for a Poetry Carnival came from Richard Watkins, Deputy Head of English at Stratford High School. The two of us had organised something similar but more modest two years before, following Richard's attendance at a D.E.S. Poetry course and an initiative to celebrate poetry nationally launched by Michael Rosen and others.

Once again we set out with modest hopes, but the offer of a grant of £4000 from David Hart, Literature Officer of West Midlands Arts, led us to be more ambitious. The offer was conditional upon Warwickshire providing £2000. In fact, the local education authority has provided much more than that through in-service training money.

The money was spent principally on a series of writer-residencies:

Kendell Smith:	Stratford High Etone School, Nuneaton St Paul's C.E. Combined, Leamington Aylesford, Warwick
Amryl Johnson:	Rugby High Knightlow C.E. Middle, Stretton-on-Dunsmore
Oscar Frank:	Cashmore Middle, Leamington
Barrie Wade:	Studley High and local feeder schools

Day workshops took place as follows:

Gareth Owen:	Henley Junior and Infant
Averil Redman:	A number of schools in Warwickshire.

In addition, money was spent on a tour of sixteen Warwickshire schools by "Words Alive", a programme of poetry readings by Barry and June Wilsher, and on the printing and publication of this anthology.

When we launched the idea of a Poetry Carnival at a crowded meeting at Books for Students in March, 1989, I think we saw it as something of a "last fling" before the closing over the National Curriculum waters. However, our worst fears were not realised. On the contrary, poetry has featured prominently in the working party proposals for the English curriculum 5–11, and there can now be no doubt that they will be an important part of the 11–16 proposals.

Other events that took place during the Carnival were:

Course, Approaches to Poetry through Drama (led by Gordon Vallins at South Warwickshire College)

Poetry dinner with readings at South Warwickshire College Training Restaurant

Poetry day for two hundred plus children at Stratford Civic Hall

Evenings for parents and children

Videos of events

Acknowledgements

I should like to thank as strongly as I can the following:

Sarah Davies for undertaking much of the initial organisation

Jim Layton and the Warwickshire Inter-Cultural Support Service for all their help with the writer residencies

Lys Bradley, Jane Naylor and Molly Pickles for reading, editing, suggesting, etc.

Richard Watkins for his quiet support at a time when he could so easily have diverted me to "more important matters", and for his support for poetry at all times.

Above all, to David Hart and West Midland Arts for their generous support.

David Howe

Contents

Footnote

Poems include the author's name when supplied and legible. There is work written (or in the case of the very youngest, transcribed) by children aged from four and a half through to eighteen. Teachers' work is included too, though not as much as we would have liked, and a few poems from parents and grandparents.

The reader can deduce, if (s)he wishes, the age and status of our authors.

Families – and Other Folk

Without You

Without you Dad,
There would be no-one
To shout at me or everyone!
To shout at the dog when she
Goes in the bin,
Or say to you stop making that din.
Without you there would be no-one
To cuddle when you come home from work.
No-one to tell really awful jokes!

Peter Atkinson

Grandad

So young and yet so old,
Full of knowledge and wisdom,
Yet love is at heart.

Joanne Hocken

Marriage

Cars screeched to a halt outside the church.
Door slammed, stilettos clicked.
Women gossiped, criticising other's clothes.
"Do you like my hat, I bought it specially?"
"Oh, it's . . . different!" Men swaying slightly.
Breath smelling of whisky or rum.
They all filed into the church.

The church bell rang out. Glistening in the sun.
People stopped to admire her shiny exterior.
Inside, feet shuffled,
Impatient children asked, "How long now mummy?"
The bridegroom glanced round anxiously.
Then checked his watch. Tick, tock, tick, tock.
Five minutes. Ten minutes. Where was she?

"Doooo!" The 'Wedding March' began.
The bride walked slowly down the aisle,
Meekly awaiting her destiny.
The older generation whispered furtively,
"Well, would you wear a dress like that?"
As the bride in a long cream dress, slit
to her thigh.
Made her way to the altar.

"Oh," snivelled her mother, "doesn't she just look like
Princess Diana?"
The bridegroom's mouth brimmed into a bright smile.
Vicar appeared looking like a wet weekend in Paris.
Mournful and depressed. Perhaps his marriage,
Had hit the rocks!
He began to say his lines.
Sounding as he looked — noncommittal!

"Do you . . . take thee . . . to be your lawful wedded husband?"
"I do." she smiled.
His face relaxed. Relief obvious.
"Do you . . . take thee . . . to be your lawful wedded wife?"
"I do!" he grunted.
Prospective mothers-in-law wept silently into their
handkerchiefs.
The fathers-in-law looked slightly the worse for drink.

The bells pealed out — Ding Dong!
Revealing to all.
That the couple would live in happy harmony.
For the rest of their lives.

Hazel Smith

Baby

Jenny Furniss
Happy baby,
Alert baby,
Always had hiccups,
Born on November 5th,
Was she frightened of
the fireworks?

Six–year–old

Baby Brother

It was a hot summer holiday from school
Mum was going to have a baby
In a way I felt happy
In a way I felt sad
I felt happy, a new baby in the family.
But sad mum would have to stay in hospital
I would go and see her though
One morning I woke only to find my Grandma was there
Mum was in hospital!
I wondered if it was a boy or girl
I wouldn't mind if it was either
We waited all day!
And just as we were having tea
Dad rang up
It's a boy!
Three girls and a boy
Now there was a boy, a grandson
Next day we went to see him and mum I went with my other grandma.
There he was asleep in his cot
Wrinkled a bit like a monkey.
On Saturday we fetched him and mum.
Well he grew up

And Jonathan's first word was tata meaning tractor
Now he's four and goes to school
He's not sweet anymore!

Miriam Paget

My Mom had the Baby

We went to see him
I was shaking,
No trembling.
I was shaking so much I thought that
I would drop him.
I was so happy.
I was tingling all over.
His tiny eyes were closed so tight.
My dad was so proud.
I wanted to stay there, looking a him
for ever and ever till . . .

HE WOKE UP.

What a noise.

Perhaps it wants a drink.
It doesn't.
Just then it shut up.
Thank goodness.

We went home.
I felt very sad.
Perhaps he's lonely without me.
I'm lonely without him and mom.

Even if he does make a noise.

Lisa Hodson

Haiku

My brother.
Like some dynamite,
He has a very short fuse,
I make myself scarce.

James Higgins

My Uncles

My uncles are fun.
One uncle goes to Africa every year
My other uncle goes to Stratford every day.

Lucy Foster

Needlemaker

The sweating workmen
Red faced
Near the white hot furnace
The room is dim lit
Flames and coal
Glow red, yellow and orange
His hands are scalded
Aching and bloodstained
As he takes the flowing needles
Out of the furnace
With his rusty shovel.

David Donelan

My Teddy Bear

My teddy bear just sits there
Looking at me
And my teddy bear just sits there
And looks at me
I wish my bear could play with me.

Bruce Webster

A Teddy Boy

An advert for Crown paints,
Luminous cans mixed into one,
A fairground at night,
Leaning against a lamp post
Wielding a chain,
Wondering about his knuckle dusters,
An evil stranger,
Jiving in the coffee bars,
Loving to show off.

Simon Dickason

My Uncle Charles

On my sixth birthday
My uncle Charles was in a coma.
He was eighty-seven years old.
It was not fair him lying there.
He was so helpless.
He had to be fed by someone else.
When he was young and fit he played Rugby.
He was a professional player.
He played for Swansea.
I felt mad.
Yet there was nothing I could do for him.
I felt like shaking him and saying.
Wake up.
Sometimes in his sleep.
He would say words.
I would run and think.
He was telling me something.

Richard Brannigan

The Worker

The worker is tired hot and afraid
As he sharpens the needles on his stone.
His cheeks are red hot, with sweat
Pouring down his face.

He is coughing and spluttering
Coughing and spluttering.
He longs to get home,
Away from dust, heat and noise,
Banging and clanking
Everywhere he looks there are
Tired red-faced workers
Thinking of the end of the day.

Nicola Hall

The Double Life

Joshua Bailey
Had just turned forty
And his family
Arranged a party
But for Bailey
It was a special night
A ten year old's birthday
In a forty year old's body
The mind's age was ten
The face thirty years more
He was old enough
To drink, smoke, marry
Get a job or drive a car
Yet everyone around him
Cared for him
Like a baby
His presents were toys
Things to help him

Not whisky
Funny cards, or gin
He was sung to
Played with
Not laughed at
Or joked on
He was leading two lives
The one on the outside
His appearances
And the one on the inside
His feelings and abilities
He was leading a Double Life!

Linda Oliver

Disobedience

It happened in the house,
When I cut my finger,
With a sharp knife.
They told me never to touch a knife.
I broke my promise,
I said to my mum,
I cut my finger when I fell off my bike.
She asked my brother.
I whispered to myself "oh no"
My brother said I was messing about with a knife.
Mum said "YOU NAUGHTY BOY"
Promise that you will never touch a knife again
I said to my mum "I will try my best".

Ketan

Memories

A clock ticked.
Spotless walls.
Silence.
Heels clicked on polished floor.
Sickly sweet smell,
Antiseptic.
Stench of death.
An old man wheeled in, face
White as flour
Beneath the sheets.
Terrified.
Silence.
A blanket of stillness
Man on the bed,
Not my grandad.
Some other old,
Withered person, cheek hollows
Like caverns.
A stranger,
Eyes closed, mouth half open,
Just breathing.
The ghosts of whispers
Echoed along the floor.
"Farewell".
We left. Then
Came the eternal journey
Down the never-ending motorway.
Home.
The phone shrilled. The clipped
Educated voice, full of fake sympathy,
Said quietly,
"He died,
I'm sorry."

Anon

Sensible Shoes

Inside the shop
Mum says
                she wants sensible shoes
not shiny stylish slingbacks
                she wants sensible shoes
not shiny stylish slingbacks
nor big thick blockerboots
                she wants sensible shoes
not shiny stylish slingbacks
nor big thick blockerboots
nor pretty little peeptoes
                she wants sensible shoes
not shiny stylish slingbacks
nor big thick blockerboots
nor pretty little peeptoes
nor tough sporty trainers
                she wants sensible shoes
not shiny stylish slingbacks
nor big thick blockerboots
nor pretty little peeptoes
nor tough sporty trainers
nor multicoloured moccasins
                she wants sensible shoes
not shiny stylish slingbacks
nor big thick blockerboots
nor pretty little peeptoes
nor tough sporty trainers
nor multicoloured moccasins
nor glossy green goloshes
                she wants sensible shoes

not shiny stylish slingbacks
nor big thick blockerboots
nor pretty little peeptoes
nor tough sporty trainers
nor multicoloured moccasins
nor glossy green goloshes
nor clumping clattering clogs.

Outside the shop she says
now you have sensible sh—
OO—and she suddenly
stops short as her
stiletto heel
gets stuck
inside a
pave-
ment
C
R
A
C
K

Anon

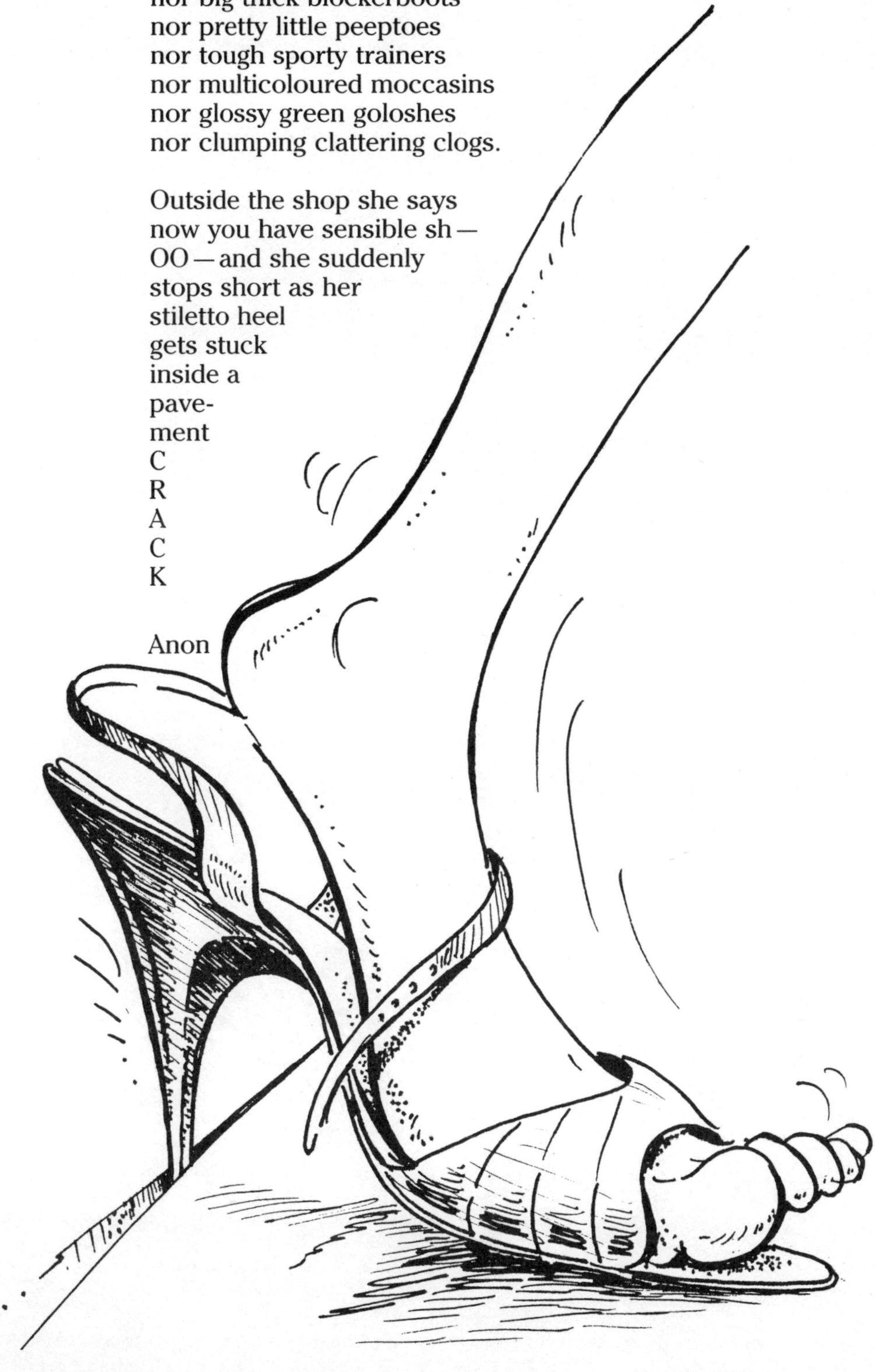

Schooldays

That's for Me

Here I am bored at school
Bored as can be
Is me

I'd rather be in the army
That's for me
Flying a harrier 'faster harry'
That's for me
Yes I'll be a pilot

In a plane
Fast and free
Wake up
It's home time!

Liam Collis

Cross Country

On a hill a face appears.
Puffing and panting.
A triumphant smile and gleaming eyes.

Cheeks as red as roses and
Bright clothes flash by.
A glimpse and they're gone.

The atmosphere is once more grey
And anticipating.
Two feet thud by, landing where
Others have gone just a moment ago.

Mud is kicked up as they strain
To carry on.

At the end the winner smiles with
A triumphant face and proud eyes
As others congratulate him.
Everyone's expression is happy and
Beads of sweat form along the
Temples of every man and woman.

Freya Blom

Playtime

Running out
Children shout
Screaming loud
Skipping round
Playing games
Football mad
Having fun
"Can I play?"
"Yes," "No."
"Not today."
"Why not?"
Kick, punch
Thump, shove
"Don't be rough."
Skip, skip
Trip, trip
Falling down
What a clown
"Hey, that's mine.
Give it back!"
Ring, ring
"Oh no," we sing
"That's the bell."
Playtime's OUT!

Emma Holmes

Morning Break

Clouds in sky's playground
pause to pull faces at me
through sunbeam railings.

Learning a Lesson

My friend, a book she asked to borrow,
And said she'd give it back tomorrow,
The next day came,
There was no book,
Only my friend,
With a guilty look.

"What have you done with my book?" I cried,
"I never had it at all," she lied.
"If you don't bring it back tonight,
You and I will have a fight."

So in the playground the next day,
My best friend was made to pay,
We fought; I won; that day at school,
My friend and I, we learned a rule.

She: "Don't borrow,"
Me: "Don't lend,"
That's my poem,
Here's the end.

Lea Insua

Friends Forever

Friends forever, okay?
Yeah, friends forever.

However the next day . . .
What you do that for?
Do what?
That.
What's that?
That's a bruise where you kicked me.
I didn't kick you anywhere.
You did.
Did not. It was that boy over there.
I'm not stupid. I wasn't born yesterday.
You kicked me.

Did not!
Did.
Did not!!!

The two frowned,
Looked around,
Then calmed down,
Smiled and said,
Friends forever, okay?
Yeah, friends forever.

Peter Row

My Dens I've Had

I remember when I had my old den.
It was my best one ever.
Now it's bashed down.
The builders did it.
My other one was good.
It was a bush and me and Stephen spied on people as
they passed.
It's all gone now, I wished it hadn't but it has
The other one we had, Stephen and I, was brill.
But, the cats ruined it with their dirty habits.
We've got more dens the only problem is the builders
are making a car park or houses there.
I don't want the builders to bash it down.

Andrew Clayton

My Future

The number seven looms threateningly above my head.
It follows me to sleep,
It's there when I awake.
I eat it for breakfast,
I play it for games.
If I fail one, I'll only get six
If it's two, five will be the number.
I am not an imbecile, but five is an idiotic number.
I will be judged by a number.
A number which is decided by people twenty years my senior.
A world dominated by numbers,
A society that adores numeracy.
A future decided by digits,
A failure decided by me.

Never!

Clare Birchall

The Battle

The rubber hit me on the neck.
I turned and scowled at Jim.
He looked at me with worried eyes
And I looked back at him.

A ruler in his hand was held.
I took one in mine too.
"A friendly fight," I said to him,
'The Battle of Waterloo.'

Jim's ruler hit the blackboard.
Mine hit the windowpane.
I wish he hadn't hit me,
For it felt much like the cane.

The fight lasted quite a while.
The teacher then came in.
"A fight in school?" she said surprised.
"Who is it? Sue and Jim!"

The fight was won by me, of course.
Who else but the Mighty Sue?
Jim gave in to my powers,
And I'm sure you would too.

The Head clapped me on the back,
The teachers said, "Well done!"
My friends cheered me on as well,
I'm so glad that I won.

There is just one little thing,
Something you should do,
Be nice to all of your friends,
And they will be nice to you.

Suzanne Hurley

His Waterloo

He was the leader of the pack,
I his right hand man.
His wish was my command.
I was his pair of fists.
No one could insult him.
No offender got away.

We were all pawns and he the king on the chessboard.
All trying to impress.
Hoping for promotion.
A stupid little incident and it was finished.
No longer was I a general.

No, I had been exiled to a life of misery and loneliness.
Wondering when he would attack my already battered ego.
Then he met his Waterloo.
His moment had come.
Now he must suffer the torment of loneliness.
Now I was the king and he the pawn.

Ian Taplin

What did you Learn at School Today?

So, what has China's National Day got to do with us?
Are they coming? No, not yet. You can see some children
With violin cases.
Knock, Knock,
And did you see that child,
Knock, Knock, Knock,
About four or five,
Vacuum cleaner twice her size?

Leave everything behind.
Take a deep breath this won't hurt one little bit
Just filling this simple riddle round and round and round

Now show us —
Hoo? Who, me? But you said —
And breathe out.

What comes next? Count them. It is
Twenty two divided by four that's five and two over,
Two with, three without, black, black, white, white, black,
Step with your partner forward and back,
Here is no milk but only water,
Hydro from the Greek, meaning water
Here is no water but only rock
If there were only water,
Fifty eight times thirteen point eight makes eight hundred
and four is that
right?
Thirty take away twenty four leaves six please help yourself.
Don't throw it away you never know when you may need it,
One triumphal march divided by four times six you can't,
Mill, mill, mill, mill,
You can, makes one whole.

Now the sacrifice.
Next year there will be only 340,000 potted plants.

Wendy Golstone

Time Present – Time Past

Canal Reflections

That which is reality on the bank,
Is a rippled and broken
Reflection in the water.
Today is real and yet it is a
Reflection of what has passed.
What is reality?
Is it today, which tomorrow
Will itself be a rippled memory?
Or is it the past although
Distant is a constant influence on the present?
Perhaps we need both, the reality
Of the present, and the reflections of the past
To complete the dreams of tomorrow.

Time

The clocks are ticking
The cogs are clicking
The ticks march like an army
The beat can drive you barmy.

Time soon is past
It goes so fast.
The time is future
It's so hard to picture.
Digital watches
A strap which clutches
Days, weeks
They're all right
Morning, noon, day, night.
Months, years
Everyone's fears
Minutes, hours.
They're on clock towers.

Daniel George

Where Are They Going?

Sitting in my little room
I hear the traffic, vroom, vroom, vroom.
Cars and lorries thundering by
Where are they going? Where ask I.

Past the field and pubs and houses
Wives and husbands back to spouses.
Bikes and buses trundling by.
Where are they going? Where ask I.

Off to offices, factories, shops.
Do they ever see the crops?
Commuters, travellers going by.
Where are they going? Where ask I.

Truckers in their heavy lorries
Chewing gum—ease their worries
Sign posts—traffic lights passing by
Where are they going? Where ask I.

Travellers in their company cars
Achievement measured in gold stars?
Where are they going? Where ask I.

Children off to schools with mothers
Girls going to meet their lovers.
Mopeds, scooters, wheeling by.
Where are they going? Where ask I.

Over the hills and far away
Is there not somewhere another way?
Rushing, hurrying, worrying by.
Where are they going? Where ask I.

M. M. Ryan

Waiting

I was waiting at the station,
The train had been delayed,
I was full of irritation
And my patience began to fade.

The waiting room was dull and dreary,
I was tired and bored stiff.
The silence really was quite eery,
Except for mumbles and a little 'sniff'.

I started tapping my hands and feet,
"Don't be annoying!" said my mum.
Dad said: "go and get something to eat."
But I just sat there, feeling dumb.

I swung my legs, read a magazine,
Had a stretch and walked around.
There was nothing interesting to be seen,
So I scuffed my shoes on the ground.

I rummaged through mum's bag for food,
I found none and slouched in my chair.
I wasn't in a really good mood
And I kept thinking "It's not fair!"

It was then the little girl came in,
Full of smiles and charm,
With lots of daisies in a tin
And draped along her arm.

She put a daisy in her hair,
And one in her left and right shoe,
I wanted to laugh but didn't dare,
Till she put one in my hair too.

She put a daisy in mum's hair
And one in dad's hair too!
They looked as though they didn't care,
And then the girl said 'boo'!

Everybody began to play
With daisies in our hair
And tho' the train had a further delay,
We really didn't care.

Jayne Cooper

Twilight Shadows

Mists . . .
Like the fallen ghosts of angels,
Trailing over the twilight earth.
The gentle whiteness of heavenly clouds,
(Made incandescent by a hidden sun)
Dull to an endless grey in mourning,
Of the dying sun.

Through the valleys and hidden hollows,
Spirits glide to a macabre dance of death.
Sighing to unknown gods.
In search of perfect nirvana,
On this evil earth.

Joy Edmonds

Lights

The festival of lights has now begun.
Colourful lights everywhere.
Fireworks in the skies
Gleaming pretty patterns up above.
A small light shoots up in the sky
Then explodes into millions of golden sparks.

And then
And then
They fade
Away
Like magic.
It all seems so beautiful so beautiful.
It's the festival of Divali.

Neelam Saran

The Seasons

Winter snowflakes fall so light,
Carpeting the earth all white.
Robins sing their song all day,
Soon the Winter's gone away.

Let's look forward now to Spring,
With lambs and flowers and birds on wing.
Singing to their hearts' content,
No sooner did it come it went!

Summer time; Oh can it be,
It's time to go to the sea,
The soft warm sand and sunny days,
Will soon fade into Autumn haze.

The leaves turn brown, green, and gold.
The days once more turn Winter cold.

Wendy Lamb

Haiku Calendar

Keen January,
frost-bladed at the earth's edge,
slices to the bone.

Bleak February
glares through baleful eyes of rooks
hunched on bare branches.

Torn clouds in the wind
go helter-skelter, pell-mell:
March rushes headlong.

Songthrush April sings
again again again its
rhapsody for Spring.

May gives its promise
with apple trees unfurling
petal flags of peace.

In egg-warming June
the nightingale's throat is still;
even leaves relax.

Simmering July:
the lime tree sizzles with bees
and bubbles over.

August stamps its foot,
strikes sparks off towering clouds,
shows its bad temper.

September stringtime:
swallows thread themselves on wires;
dangled conkers spin.

Golden October
mints its coins in plums and pears.
Leaves reflect the fire.

Dreary November:
cherry trees droop skeletal,
shrink into themselves.

December shivers
kaleidoscopic pieces
out of leaden skies.

Tennis Blues

Dust ascends
As the tennis ball hits the sun baked court.
Heads turn from side to side
In a strange ritual
As the spectators view,
Oblivious of the wrinkles hatching
Rouge strawberries enveloped in thick cream
Are accompanied by ice-cubes clinking
In a long tall glass.
The whiles blind even the darkest sunglasses
No-one cares
Summer is triumphant.

Hot and Cold

Scorching, they eat cold desserts.
Hot, they drink quenching cocktails,
Baked alaskas lie.

Signs of Summer

Sun bakes, ice-cubes clink,
Tarmac sweats, grass elongates;
Summer, at last!

Rebecca Temple

Some Summer Thoughts

Shady pond,
Open air,
Dancing sunshine,
Everywhere.

Daisy chain,
Nettles stinging,
Old trees
Ivy clinging.

Mark Honeybunn

The Long Journey

When it's the Summer holiday
We go to a place called Croyde Bay
After about ten minutes a little voice says
M . . . M . . . m—u—m
Mum stops the car
I close my eyes
Ben gets out
HE
IS
FEELING
SICK
I hate it
Every ten minutes!
And I have to put up with it
Bother!   Oh no
AGAIN!

The Train

The sound of an engine
The smell of the diesel
The banging of doors
The guard blows the whistle
The light turns green
The train starts
Clickety clack clickety clack
Clickety clack clickety clack
Whooooo
Houses, trees, cattle and
Farmers
Fields we flew past
We started to slow
Then we drew in to the
Station
The journey is over.

Craig Arnold

Slide

When you're ten years old,
The hot, sticky Summers are endless.
Collecting small, grey pebbles,
Me and my friend,
Sliding down the sea wall.

Here's the Barrel Organ man.
The monkey leaps and falls.
Spinning marbles,
Me and my friend,
And sliding down the sea wall.

The 'Sally Army's' here again,
Singing sweet hymns down on hard, stony shores,
Longing for a tambourine,
Me and my friend,
Sliding down the sea wall.

A firey sun becomes deep, golden, rust.
Dusk soaks the beach.
Quick, catch the hot chestnut man.
Gather up buckets and spades,
And me and my friend, take one last
Slide down the sea wall.

Rochanne Beebee

September Holiday

Waves lapped quietly on the beach
Shingle crunched under our feet
Clear blue sky up above
The kind of day I really love.

Distant ships on the horizon
Gulls circled round screeching and crying
No other people, no hub-bub
The kind of day I really love.

Eyes looked down to inspect the stones
Looking for treasures to take home
Shells and pebbles all looked good
The kind of day I really love.

Ashley Ballard

Autumn

It is Autumn
The trees are brown, red and yellow
The sky is fluffy ice-cream
Pinky marshmallow on the dotty blue canopy.

Watching Autumn

Watch the leaves as they fall to the ground.
Watch the trees as they swirl all around.
Watch the flowers as they droop to the ground.
Watch the frost in the dark, dark town.

Watch the fires blazing very high.
Watch the fireworks shooting through the sky.
Watch the days they get shorter and shorter.
Watch the rivers with freezing water.

Philip Malkin

November

No leaves on the deciduous trees.
No short socks in the cold.
No ice-creams in the winter.
No insects under the ground.
No playing out late in the dark.
No butterflies flying in the sky.
No ice-lollies in the winter.
No birds in the trees.
No crops in the fields.
No animals in the street.
November.

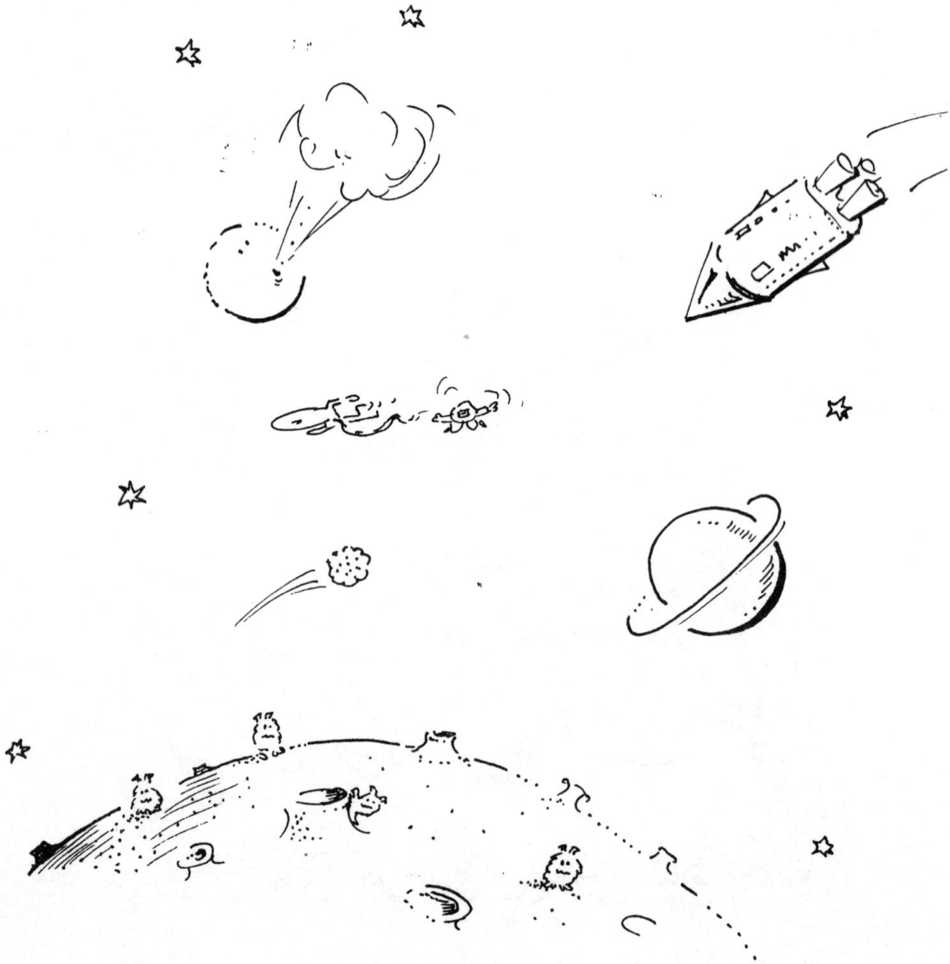

Our World— and Beyond

Traffic

Noxious fumes escape,
Fluctuating clouds of chaos,
Erupting from the mechanical monsters.
Like motorised chainsmokers,
They emit their haze of doom.
Variegated vessels,
Careering along the toxic lattice of grey,
Once dull network,
Now kaleidoscopic madness.
The monsters roar and growl,
Slowly chugging back to life,
Conducted by the rhythmic stiletto heel.
Other mechanisms join the ensemble,
Signalled in by a flickering green.
Growling monsters of agony.
Incongruent size and velocity,
Varying degrees of dissonance,
Cascading from the moaning mechanisms.
The conducting stiletto heel loosens its timing
Buried in the meandering horde of commuters.
Like demented percussionists,
They drown the master melody.
Intermingled with the bleating pelican.
Rolling roads of colour,
Enhanced by the mechanical orchestra.
Time passes like a rocketing echo,
Once more to overcome the silence this maybe.

Tim Cowley

GRR

Flight

Electronic Wizardry fitted everywhere
Switches, knobs, dials
To
H.U.D., Radar, Infra Red targeting
Jaguars to Tornados,
Harriers to F.1s,
All sorts of shapes as well
Curved, bent, streamlined,
Straight, sharp, aerodynamic
Jet engines, ram engines
Vertical take off
Supersonic
It really is fantastic, exciting
Exhilarating,
It really is great!

A Tribute to Steve Biko

What did you do?
You did not deserve such treatment.
You fought for our rights.
You died trying to help us.
Murderers, why do you hate us?
What have we done to you?
Colour is only skin deep.
Split us open and we're the same as you.
We're not like rock,
We don't have "BLACK" running through us.

You died for your beliefs.
How many more people must be killed,
Until they see the truth.
Eternity?
But the killings still go on,
And on and on . . .

Anon

The Dissident

The red flag wraps tighter,
And the oppression begins to tell.
Being rejected from society,
Because of your view.
If the opinion does not fit
Neither do you.

Trodden on by the authorities,
What they say goes.
Like a modern day Christ,
A martyr to trial,
A trial where there can be but one victor,
Not you.

Removed from your way of life.
Taken away to be forgotten about,
To a domain where freedom in any form,
Is but a memory.
Where solitude keeps discipline,
Better than any fire-arm could.
Where dejection and hostility breed freely,
Setting in like flies on a carcass,
And hope begins to fade.

In only the strongest the will survives,
To continue fighting if freed,
To carry on banging your head against the wall,
But some do,
In the hope that one day,
The cement might crumble,
And a brick dislodge.

Matthew Kearsey

The Creation

God thought he would make a planet
First he made the day and night
Each was opposite of the other,
One was dark and one was light.

Next he made the heaven and earth
He put the heaven above the sky
The sky was beautiful blue
The heaven was incredibly high.

Now, the earth looked very bare,
So God made grass and trees,
The grass was bright green
The new ocean rippled.

Now the earth looked very good.
To generate heat he made a sun
The sun was surrounded by stars
Making the moon was really fun.

The Earth looked good but still bare.
So he made many animals and birds,
And rabbits, bees and hares
And elephants that come in herds.

Now God was tired but happy,
He was joyous. He made woman and man
But, he didn't have anything to tend his place
"I know" he thought "people can!"

God did not want to do any more,
So he had a rest
They and creatures lived in peace,
God knew he had done his best!

Scott McGaffney

Small World

Tommy throws his crisp packet on the ground,
All together now,
Sister Jane sprays her hair all around,
All together now,
Dad throws the rubbish in the lane,
All together now,
The manager tips waste down the drain,
All together now,
Scientists use the sea as a tip,
All together now,
Men in Russia make a slip,
All together now,
Rain causes all the trees to die,
All together now,
There's a hole appearing in the sky,
All together now?

Karen Daniels

A Confusion of Images

Light trickles down, tingling, a shower through my mind;
Water flows in the background, sparkling, bubbling,
in my imagination.

She flicks back her hair, a shadow, an image
And walks around a fountain of pearls that is not there.
The silk of hallucination caresses my skin,
Then softly, slithers to the floor.
A snake of illusion wraps around my brain,
Hissing inspiration in the darkness of my life.
A picture forms, hazy, misty. A tiger stalks its prey.
The leap, majestic and silent into the still waters of the deep,
The swimmer emerges, shattering the surface, gasping for air.

She steps out of the water, treading on the crunching,
glittering fragments of glass;

I'm Black! So What?

I'm black!
So what?
I'm proud to be black.
You should learn that.
I'm no different to you.
I still drink and eat.
I still wash and sleep.
I'm black!
So what's it to you.

I'm black!
So what?
I breathe the same air.
And wear the same clothes.
I speak the same language.
And I still walk the same streets.
And live on the same earth.
I have the same feelings.
I laugh and cry.
I live and die.

Clare Mason

So Far and Yet So Near

I look into the sky so far and yet so near,
Stars made up from enlarged particles of dust,
Nothing is heard, the heaven of complete silence,
The angriness of the sun that burns like fire,
The desolation of different worlds that no-one inhabits,
Pale, gentle softness of the green Milky Way,
Longing for life, for feelings, emotions,
The Earth surrounded by clouds of thought,
A whipped creamy spiral of Venus,
I looked up into the starry night,
So far and yet so near.

Joanne Hocken

Space

Space; dark, eerie and silent,
Man's dream to explore,
The rocket his transportation,
Imagination his friend.

Space; to venture forth,
Risking life and limb,
All that preparation, is it worth it?
Is there really something there?

Space; a solemn and awesome sight,
The orange glazed sun,
The stipple of stars,
The grey and mourning moon.

Space; binded by millions of stars,
Filled with glory,
Filled with devastation.
Is there no end to its beauty of colours?

Space; of which man has many questions to ask,
Some may soon be answered,
Some may never be answered.
Time is the element and what now lies
Beyond is a mystery.

Richard Elbaz

Astronaut

A ll you eight will go to
S pace to take a look at
T he moon, you will orbit a
R ound the earth and be the first men
O n the planet.
N eil, you will descend first
A nd you eight will explore the surface
U se your instruments and
T ry to find us a new world.

David Wood

One Small Step for Man

One small step for man
One giant step for mankind
It's good on the moon.

Hi There, Satellite

Hi there, satellite, orbiting in outer space.
What do you see of the human race?
Aborigines carrying out traditions.
And nomads wearing turbans in Saudi Arabia.
I see people on walking holidays near the Grand Canyon.
I also see maize by the Mississippi river.
And grey seals on the coast of Alaska.
Elephants working energetically in the Burma hills.
And Nuclear Power in Chicago.
Citrus fruits fresh from Portugal,
Ready for us to eat.
I see Torriden near the highlands of Scotland.
OOOOH! coffee from Cuba!
Ostriches leaping energetically across
The Nambia deserts with mighty bounds!
And excited holidaymakers on the
Barbados coasts.
Tigers by the Indian holy river the Ganges.
I also see Mont Fuji puffing its steaming pipe.
That's what my eye in outer space
Has to report on the human race.

Colin Heinink

Shortage of Food

All over the world
People are dying of starvation,
We've got to mention
About the starvation
To richer nations.

People are dying and babies are crying,
Children are pleading and old people sighing.

If only we could give more money,
They don't have much to eat only bread and
Honey,
It is serious not funny,
Oxfam gives money,
People need to help both man and lady

People are dying babies crying
Children are pleading old people sighing.

Richard Hawkes

All Kinds of Animals

In the Wild

Horses galloping freely,
Mane tossing,
Tail swishing behind,
Over the hills and dale,
Jumping over running streams,
Hooves clopping on stony grounds,
Tundering past little rabbits, as if saying:
Faster, faster must go faster,
Trees and bushes flying past,
But the wild horse will not stop,
Until he reaches his destination.

Nina Sims

Tiger

Not seen by all eyes,
But seen by the swaying grass,
A pounce and a kill.

Humpback Whale

Streamlined and gentle,
As blue as the sea itself,
Crying its sorrow.

Bird of Paradise

Bright and cheerful,
Floating on the air alone,
Seen by man and enemy.

The Wind

Teasing at your hair,
Edged with the chill of nature,
Not seen but heard, felt.

The Acorn

An acorn so small,
Just a shell for protection,
Yet so full of life.

Three Children Reflect on the Death of Animals

When Katie came to my house
Hannibal died.
Carl was cross
He blamed Wendy.
But he just died really
In his little box my
Hannibal.
I was sad.

Paul

I had a cat
A lady cat
She was called Tig.
She got poorly.
My Mum gave her
      some tablets
And medicine.
But she lay down
   on the floor
And died.

Natalie

What a lot of cats
      get killed.
Because they run
      out on to the road.
Cars, motorbikes and
      lorries
All seem to dislike
      cats
I wonder why.

Sean

Non-replaceable

Maybe you wouldn't have taken his place.
But you did.
So different, so unlike him,
You were a misfit,
But, your shyness, the way you looked.
Sharp dusky fur just like Scamp's.
You barked and shrieked,
Acted high and mighty, but I could see through you.
Not like him, he listened when told.
You came and curled up close to me.
But don't think you've won me over.
The others love you, enjoy your warmth,
But I don't think I do.
That glimmer in your eye—
Love, not spite.
Maybe I could just be your friend
I know inside you're not here to take his place
You're just here to be cared for and loved,
But Scamp's memories live on.

Anon

A Kitten

Smooth and cuddly,
Soft and furry,
Squashy and cute,
A kitten's like this.

Amarpreet

Without You

Without you I won't
be able to lift you out
of your cage or, let
you run up my sleeve.
I love you, you are
my one, and only mouse.
I am glad you live in
a cage because the cat
would not get you.
I am glad I called you
Samantha, the mouse.

Barnaby Jones

The Otter

As it glides
And it slides
Silky, smooth and soft

Watching me walk
He darts away
Among the rushes
Into his hole

Jumpy, bouncy springy
He flies over the land
Always alert
Quick and active

That's the Otter for me!

Ruth Rowland
(Written after a TV music
session on the otter and making
music.)

The Cat

As white as the snow,
It sits on the fence alone,
Watching the birds fly.

James Dyson

The Gerbil

Runs fast
Smooth fur.
Brushed back.
Spikey hair.
Wonder what he's doing there.

Wayne

Little Pig

Little pig
Pink and fat
In your little pigsty
When you get much bigger
You won't think much of that.

Tina Salisbury

The Hare

Hares are fast,
Hares are brown,
Hares make their homes
Underground.

Thomas Griffiths

Lambs

Lambs say baa
Cows say moo
They don't talk
Like me and you

The Hen

A little hen
Pecks over the farm
Thinking about other things

Beverley Masterman

Our Cat

I have a black cat
She is quite fat
She's nice to see
But you have to leave her be
When she's on the
Settee.

Alan

Old Dog

Old dog,
Lies by the fence with head on paws,
His brown-grey skin twitches as a bee lazily passes,
Dreaming,
Dreaming of younger years,
Chasing a butterfly,
Catching a ball,
Knocking a dustbin to the ground,
Bang,
The front door closes,
His long soft ears prick, and fall,
He heaves his heavy body from the dust,
And stretches his creaking joints in the afternoon heat,
He goes to investigate,
But soon wanders back,
And falls asleep.

David Daise

Witches' Brew

One wiggly worm,
Two tasty toads,
Three thick thumbs,
Four flies eyes,
Five fat frogs,
Six slimy sausages,
Seven smelly socks,
    Simon's spell:
Humpty, bumpty, ping, pong,
Humpty, bumpty, bumpty, bong.
Footy, booty, booty
    —POP!

Bobdog

Most dogs
Love to eat
Munchy biscuits, tins of meat;
Juicy bones to crack and crunch
Your Dad's socks,
The Sunday lunch.
But not Bobdog!
Oh no!
He's an odd dog
Is our Bobdog
He likes;
Eating plaster off the wall
Chewing the paper in the hall
Curried teabags, frozen rolls,
Wire wool,
Flowerpots,
Plastic bowls!
He's an odd dog
Is our Bobdog.
Is he a bit like your dog?
Most dogs
Like to chase
Next door's cat all over the
  place,

Sniff other dogs' bottoms
Bark and growl.
Chase their tails
Whine and howl.
But not Bobdog;
Oh no!
He's an odd dog
Is our Bobdog.
He likes;
Chinese food and watching the
  telly.
Dozing, dreaming,
Scratching his belly.
Eating chocolates through the
  post.
A cup of tea,
A slice of toast.
He's an odd dog
Is our Bobdog.
Is he a bit like your dog?

Campbell Perry

Goldfish

Goldfish in the pond
Look like metal submarines
But opening their mouths.

Christina

The Otter

Showing off again,
The otter swimming on its back—
Teeth sharp as razors.

Simon

A Dog in the Classroom

Jumping, playful, happy, bright,
Coloured Ginger, cream and white,
Excitable, panting, sweetfaced, slim,
Everyone trying to pamper him,
Tongue out, wet, and glistening pink,
He's a happy dog, I think,
Eyes are gleaming and dark brown,
He smiled a lot, he didn't frown,
Ears propelling side to side,
He didn't try to run and hide,
He's not short, but he's not tall,
Happy shining face looks up,
He looks very like a little pup,
Little spikes peep out of his paws,
Sammy stretching out his claws.

Emma Feely

Fish

I have got some fish
They bubble in the water
But they do not talk

Sian Beard

Rabbit on the Loose

It was time for me to put the rabbit back in his hutch.
"Arnold, Arnold," I called.
Mostly he would come running out of his hiding place.
But today there was no sign of him.
I went to have a look.
I looked everywhere.
Behind the shed,
In the shed,
Under the holly bush.
Everywhere.
But do you think I could find that rabbit?
No such luck.
I started to panic.
My heart started to beat really fast.
I was so scared.
"I think I know," I thought to myself.
We had a wooden fence.
There were a couple of planks of wood bent around,
  and a rabbit-sized hole.
I decided to call dad.
"What," he said. "I told you to block that hole up."
Mum told me to make some notes and
  put them in everybody's letter box.
The notes said this;

> Escaped
> Black rabbit
> Please ring 78664
> or, 79 Murray Road.

But before I had finished the last one, the doorbell rang,
Mum answered it.
Mum called dad. “Come here quick.”
Dad came,
Mum said
“Thankyou,”
And shut the door.
The man had found Arnold and brought him back.
He knew who he belonged to.
Arnold had blood all over his chest.
The man kept rabbits and Arnold had had a fight with one of them.
We cleaned him up and he was fine.
We didn’t need to call the vet.
He was such a strong rabbit.

Eva Majcherczyk

Feelings and Reflections

Poet's Lament

Since early October
I've not been quite sane;
A demon's possessed me
And captured my brain.

I'm thinking in meters,
In tempo and time,
My thoughts are all geared
To scan and to rhyme.

I lie in bed dreaming
Of Haiku and such
And even when waking
I'm not up to much

For I am obsessed and
I cannot control
The demon that's taken
This dominant role.

This demon has struck
Right across Warwickshire;
There's scarcely a place
That is immune, I fear.

You ask, "What has happened?"
"Why has this occurred?"
It's Poetry Carnival—
Hadn't you heard?

A.W.

Things Could Be Worse

If you haven't got your bag
On the way to the chip shop
BUT IT GETS EVEN WORSE
If you haven't got your purse
When you're being served in a
  chip shop
BUT NOW FOR THE GRUESOME BIT
You don't know what to do.
You're red with embarrassment
Everyone's looking
So you have to go home again
In the pouring wet rain.

Kim Morris

Things Could Be Worse

A blackbird could eat my rabbit.
My dentist could pull all my
Teeth out.
A poltergeist could come to our
School.
BUT IT GETS EVEN WORSE . . .
We could get a power cut during
Neighbours.
My wheel could fall off my bike
When I'm in the middle of
Nowhere.
A clown's red plastic nose could
Get stuck on his real nose.
BUT NOW COMES THE GRUESOME
BIT . . .
They could bring flares back into fashion.

Julie Robinson

Poems in Emotion
Happiness

Happiness is a rainbow,
It tastes like treacle pudding with warm thin custard,
Happiness smells like Honeysuckle after it's rained,
Happiness sounds like a waterfall,
It looks like a field of red, blue and yellow
Flowers,
Happiness feels like a warm soft comfortable bed
While the wind is howling and the rain is pattering outside.

A Stable

New water trough,
New bale of straw,
New saddle rack,
Clean water,
New bag of oats,
No feeding bucket!

Dawn Rose

The Writer

She is the one who sits and thinks.
When Miss says *write* our pens race into gear,
Twist through letter loops and word chicanes
With mids tight-bunched and hammering to overtake.
It is as if in pole-position she has stalled.
Her brow is radiator furrowed.
She judders at her desk
and I can see that Miss is trying not
To lean across to give a push.
By the lesson's end her littered page
Shows fragments of tyretread
Patterned into asphalt
And yet

She is the one who stands and reads
Next day while we sit breathless,
Whose words splash coloured images
Brilliant as petrol spilled in puddles
That we passed along our way.

In the Dark

In the dark I lie there,
Awake, listening for sounds.
I hear a door slam shut.
I hear the television talking.
I hear a lady out walking on the path outside.
A car starts,
An owl hoots.
A tree silhouetted by the moon.
My wardrobe door creaks open.
Dark shadows in the room,
I hope it's morning soon.

Hannah Westwood

The House

The house stands desolately
Amidst spooky hollows of trees,
Apparitions move silently,
Not disturbing
The tense atmosphere,
Filling the rooms with a
Thunderous silence.
The midnight clock strikes.
Memories of centuries of
Dank history
Breaking the frigid air
as a butcher, wielding
an unfriendly cleaver
chops, cannibalistically
Into soft raw flesh.
The pressure intolerable,
As miserable ghosts
Continue haunting the hallowed halls.
Halls as hallowed to the house
as the sanctuary of sleep
after the immortal happenings
of All Hallows Eve,
The ghosts become,
for another year
Immaterial to the cold house.

The desolate house is lonely.

Elizabeth Murray

Leaving

Your expression is understanding,
Calm, impassionate.
Where is the anger that I felt?
Why don't you hate those white collars who have ruined me?
Our children will see a grown man cry.
A man too thin,
Shabby, distant.
A man who hangs his head in shame,
Who avoids people's eyes.
A man with no self respect,
No bubbling confidence and pride.
Just a man who queues once a week,
A man who often drinks,
Swears and beats the ones he loves,
The ones who stand by him,
The ones who understand,
The ones who suffer.
I've seen it all before,
One hundred and one times and the case is always the same,
So, I'll be leavin' now,
Because you don't deserve all this pain,
I'm better off alone with nothing,
Than sharing my nothing with you.

Clare Birchall

My Imagination

Tiger roaring in a cage,
Bones crunching underfoot,
But I'm not scared,
No, I'm not scared!
The tigers are the wind,
And the bones are leaves
Crisp and stiff under me,
So, I'm not scared,
No, I'm not scared!

Caroline Leeson

Autumn

The
A
u
t
u
m
n
wind
What is this red and gold carpet?
It is the leaves, it is the leaves.
What is this musty smell?
It is the air of Autumn, the air of Autumn.
Who are you?
I am me and you are you, are you.
But who are you? Who echoes round me?
Who's cold and howls?

I am the wind, I am the wind.

Caroline

Church

Church church
With pictured windows
And a bell on top,
Church church
With pebbled walls
With Jesus on a cross,
A big tall spire
On top of the church
Right up in the air,
Church church
How do you manage
With all those things
Stuck to you?
I wouldn't like to be
A church.

Jack Hancocks

Death

A graveyard full of graven images,
A gypsy garbed in gaudy garments.
Life is here, but hidden,
Locked in stone, but no-one
holds the key.
He sits, such a contrast!
Gargoyles sneer with screwed-up eyes,
Nosegays crouch over inscriptions,
Masquerade their final words.
His feet rustle the leaves before him,
"Listen," he whispers in his husky
voice, but to whom or what?
Maybe he holds the key, and twists
it in locked hearts.
They scream in agony, too late
Life, passed for them,
Not a word!
All must now be still.

Jonathan Lunn

An Ode to the Vain

Amused. The pride of those with nothing.
The 'tight trousers brigade' come, swaggering,
Leaving victims strewn: asphyxiated—
The wearers immune to their own death drug.

Laid back, hair back, jacket back—stagger back.
Dark glasses deceiving only themselves.
"Hi gang, my gang, girl bang, thankyou mam":
slam!
Amused. The pride of those with nothing.

Helen Getlevog

The Ornithologist

Bird watcher extraordinaire — lying down,
Hanging down, glasses down,
Wearing frown.
Distant whistle from a wolf, baring teeth,
On the hearth, macho beef, holding sheath.

Waiting for the prey to walk within its way.
Wanton day, 'jug jug' pay, forced to lay.
Now inside its snare, hanging up, gripping hair.
See me glare, greasy bear — pathetic dare.

Helen Getlevog

The Blues

I'm slouching down the street, I've got those mean old Christmas
blues.
I'm starin' at the floor I've got nothin' to gain nothin' to
lose.
The world's grey and dull sounds never lull, I'm back down
starin'
at ma shoes.

Oh yeah I've got those Christmas blues
Oh yeah I've got those mean old Christmas blues.

Haven't got a job I can rarely find two or three bob, nobody will
listen to my views.
Nothin' to live for, nothin' to die for, I'd like to be rich but
I can't choose.
I'm broke and I can change that, I just got to keep myself
amused.
I'm 43 still pickin' fags off the street.
Oh yeah those Christmas blues,
Oh yeah those mean old Christmas blues.

Thomas Salmon

What Does the Word "Friend" Mean?

Friend is a word that I
have never quite understood
Does it mean unselfish and
Positive? well it means
quite the opposite to me.

A friend is a person
who picks you up in the
dark and loneliness and
then like a piece of wood
on fire it glows to give
you warmth and make you
feel safe. It takes complete
control of you and then
it gently blows out and
leaves you alone. It leaves
you in the same situation
as before.

I have never tasted friendship
but it smells and seems
beautiful to me. But when the
word "Friendship" comes into action
somehow it does not bond
together to form what it should.

Who am I? am I a ghost,
an evil ghost whom people
cannot see, even if they can see
but they can't make friends
with an evil ghost.

I wonder who put this
coat of evil or rejection
on me. Whoever did, I am
sick and tired of it.
I want to take it off
but to make it possible
to do this, I need the
helpful hand of a friend.

Kuljit Khehra

Show Me How

Show me how to touch the stars of the moonlit sky.
Show me how to see the wind whistling in the trees.
Show me how to smell the birds flying over the trees.
Show me how to hear the rainbow made out of wild
flowers.
Show me how to hear the sun burning down on
the lake.
Show me how to smell the water of the lake.
Show me how to taste the moon shining down on
the land.

Paula

Listen

I like people humming because it's so soft and gentle.
I love the disco listening to the music to dance to loud or soft.
Who likes listening to paint on a paintbrush on some paper?
Guess who likes water running out of a tap me that's who.

It's me who likes the birds in the trees and the slam of the door

BUT I COULDN'T IF I WAS DEAF.

Emma B.

In the Library

Miss Goodman stands behind the polished conter
Stamping books.
Her hair is frizzed and orange
And she wears a face
That's somewhere between
A smile and smirk.
—You've got a lot of books today.
I hand across the ten pence fine
That otherwise I would have spent
(on polo mints and aniseeds).
The library smells of old castles
And the oily heat
That seeps from radiators.
As always
The strange old lady
In the plastic pixie hat is there.
Her plastic bag is full of books.
She ranges shuffling up and down
Her eyes up searching the spines
In the section marked Romance.
On the wall is a peeling poster
Warning you of AIDS;
—Don't take the risk, it says.
Does that apply to everything?
Next to The Little Theatre Guild
Tells me Habeas Corpus is a funny play,
I'll have to go some night
Because my mum belongs.
I make for Stories:
The cars roar up and down
The Henley High Street.
In here I'm in a hundred different worlds.
Retrieving magic rings in Middle Earth,
Or in the fifth year at Saint Clare's
Bolting the midnight feast
With Isobel and Pat
Before Mamselle comes round
To call lights out;
And then again I swoop through clouds
Above the Dardanelles,
The flack snows round my Hurricane

But someone taps the morse code out
—We will be back
Don't worry mother
We'll be back
With blood and death and high adventure
Carried 'neath our arms,
Amongst the rain dashed faces
And the windows full of lights
And dummies staring at the streets,
OH mother do not worry
I'll be back,
I do this every week now
And it hasn't killed me yet.

Garaeth Owen and pals;
Sally Faulkner
Jenny Owen
Helen Goldthorpe
Alex Camer
Ronald Clinton
Stephen Woodream

Poetry is...

(Some definitions by pupils at a secondary school)

A window into the fantasy world of the human brain.

Solid facts entwined into ideas of fantasy.

Something to which you relate your life and personal experiences.

A step into another world.

The poet's imagination put on to paper.

The writer's own thoughts and imagination.

Different for everyone that reads it.

Never ending.

A collection of words which describe a person's innermost thoughts and feelings.

Words and phrases woven together to make a cloth of thought.

What you want it to be; people have different opinions.

Poetry stretches your imagination to the full.

Elementary Canal

Listen to the noise of the boat
Vibrations, chugging.
It's almost a pulse beat
Juddering.
It swishes and clatters
We're not moving now
It's almost died out
Ticking over . . .
Whirring.

Are we moving, Caroline?
I think we're stuck!
The engine's straining
"Do you want us to push
on the long pole?"
The boat sways
From side to side.
There's a judder . . .
Tensions at the wheel,
Recriminations are heard
From skipper and mate.

They said it wouldn't get rough.
Ros is out of the kitchen,
So it must be serious.
We're stuck in the mud
We're stick in the muds
Quick . . . I've got a poem coming on!

He's coming with a pole,
It's probably never happened before.
Hooray, Malcolm the great boatman
Has set us free.
"Would you like some tea?"
Scones, clotted cream
And strawberry jam
I'm glad the others aren't here!

I'll have one to start with
I'm not a big eater.
Is it jam on cream
Or cream on jam
A bit of density there,
Yes, a cross curricular scone.
After our ordeal
We deserve this!

They'll be wondering where we are,
I hope Dorothy is O.K.
That sign says,
"Caution — Deep Mud"
Look what they've walked through!

Itinerary for a Prospective Canal Journey

The longboat waiting at Thrupp.
Thrupp where 'The Boat' is said
To serve Mords in season,
Morchella esculenta.
A delicacy denied
Travellers on Dabchick.
Ahead of us lies Hampton Gay,
A misnomer. One headstone
Poignantly noting the eve
Of Christmas eighteen seventy
Four. Nine coaches of the train
Crashed into the icy cut,
Thirty four watery graves,
Forever make mockery
Of the name of Hampton Gay.
For a mile the Cherwell forms
The navigational course,
Shipton Weir and Baker's lock,
Hazardous in times of flood.
Pinsey Bridge is round the bend.
Through Pigeon's Lock, Kittlington

A stroll away on the right.
Now under Old Brighton Bridge,
Drifting on to Northbrook Lock.
Bridges — Dashwoods, Highbush, Cleeves.
Lower Heyford is ahead,
Cars, husbands, homes and Monday.

N.B. Quote from 'Places of Interest' — 'The Boat' serves Morrells, meals and snacks.

Morrels are an edible fungus — how interesting to serve a local delicacy in the pub. Think they've misspelt it — check — Yes only one "l". Deflation time comes when on arrival at Thrupp the pub sign announces 'MORRELLS ALES' — Ah Well! I'd rather be au fait with gastronomic delights and show my ignorance about breweries and the swilling of Ale . . . I think.

The Natural World

Sunset

Red and gold meet
And mingle into orange
Like coloured ink
On wet paper.
The sun is sinking
Towards the horizon's
Open jaws
With a snap the jaws close
And the sun is swallowed
As supper for the hungry horizon.
But I don't think he was satisfied
Because come morning
He spits him out!

Anita Ewing

River

Winding, blue and wet.
Glinting in the bright sunlight
Watch the river flow.

Birds

Gliding in the sky,
Flying high on air currents,
Birds are magical.

Moon

White torch in the sky
Magical, bright and gleaming
Pool of shining light.

The Snail

Slow and easily
smooth and leisurely
it slides
silent as a daydream
swaying its spirals of brown fantasy
leaving slender threads for memory
to trace
and follow later

Water

The river flowing
Through the wood it trickles
Under the bridge.

I am a Fir Tree

I am a fir tree from afar
On my head I wear a star
Around my waist a tinsel belt,
At my feet the children knelt.

Christmas presents under me
One for you as you can see
Christmas morning when light is dawning
Down the stairs come children yawning.

They open their eyes in surprizing wonder
As they see the gifts stacked under.
They open them at tremendous speed
Mummy says "Just what I need".

Catherine Nestor

Winter Morning

The trees
Bare
Black
Spear shaped
Spikes
Big ball
Red round
Tomato sky
Shrinking down
Sinking
Setting
Sun

Group poem from picture stimulus.
"Winter Morning" by Ted Ripley.
Age of children 5–6 years.

Garlic

Human like veins on 'fleshy' skin.
Smells like an onion, strong and tasty.
It looks like a flower bud, petals and
stalk.
Its colour is a creamy white mixed in
rose pink.
Its stalk looks like a bone.
When you peel off its shell it looks
like a mild cheese.
A smooth texture, like silk.

Joanne Lambert

Wind

Wind, Wind, comes and goes blowing every
thing all around, curling up like some
thing old,
Turning like a witch's cloak waving in
the wind,
Blowing everything off people's washing
lines then people wonder where their
washing has gone,
people turning to get their washing
Jumping and curling to catch it
from the air.

Kelly Richardson

Stunning Ice-skaters

One pair of stunning ice-skaters,
Both turning in the air,
While turning also stretching,
Like a spinning top going round.
After that they then,
Drop and stop,
Then still.
After those skaters jump back up
again and start to turn around and
around,
They then fall to the ground,
All curled up like a ball.

Alice Winstone

The Clouds

A cloud scurries across the sky
There appears a magic carpet
Up in the high
Then cloud dives down to the ground
and round
The magic carpet goes wonkey
And up and up goes the cloud
It scurries across the sky and then
It goes and drops a shower of water
It blows and scurries across the sky.

Neil Ward

The Rose

In Autumn the Rose dies slowly
and ungracefully. And is nothing
but curled up crumbled up rubbish
But Spring releases a new lease
of life. The rose steadily stretches
into one of the most lovely
flowers of the garden.

Daniel Farley

Poetry in the Science Room

The magic of a crystal
Deep beneath the seas
Is a very fantastic
experience
Like a forest with a thousand trees.

An icicle wonderland
What a beautiful sight
With all the colours of the
rainbow
Blazing colour and light.

Stephen George

Observe Closely

A twilight party of colours
The wintertime under the
sea
The inside of an oyster
shell
Where the colours play
merrily.

In the land the colour of day
Where the mermaids dance
and play
The medieval shadows are
summoning
And the witches are
cunning.

A giant peaceful forest
A mysterious bobble land
The purple headed
mountain
With no movement or
sound.

Kerri and Gaynor

In the Fields in Autumn

In the fields in Autumn
One tired and exhausted farmer walks into his house after
the harvest.
In the fields in Autumn
Two birds are singing softly and beautifully ready to fly
off to a hotter country.
In the fields in Autumn
Three new trees start spreading and stretching their
branches out.
In the fields in Autumn
Four conkers bounce and collapse off a tree.
In the fields in Autumn
Five crisp and white snowflakes show the beginning of
Winter.
In the fields in Autumn
Six pylons send electricity to our houses.
In the fields in Autumm
Seven black and white cows go into the barn to shelter
from the Winter blizzards.
In the fields in Autumn
Eight happy and contented farm workers look forward
to going home as darkness falls.

James Whittaker

Appendices

In order to present a fuller account of what took place, I have included a number of appendices: reports and letters from children, teachers and writers that together offer a kaleidoscope of impressions.

A. Accounts from three schools of their programme of events for the Poetry Carnival.

B. Accounts from pupils and teachers of the various writer residencies.

C. A writer's view.

D. Some reactions to the visits of "Words Alive": Barry and June Wilsher, and the Wilshers' tour itinerary.

E. A list of schools whose work is represented in this anthology.

But here is a final poem which is one of four written — and performed by — teachers in response to a challenge to mirror a performance based on words unconnected in terms of meaning, but having in common the ability to rhyme. The words were taken from a rhyming dictionary.

i.e.

1. embursement
   assortment
   refreshment
   deportment
2. mathematic
   acrobatic
   rheumatic
   dramatic
3. obsolescent
   phosphorescent
   acquiescent
   adolescent
4. hydraulics
   aerobics
   appendix
   heroics

Whilst it is flat, and in terms of being 'meaningful' poetry leaves much to be desired, they nevertheless proved fun to prepare and present and somewhere along the line many gained pleasure from working together and in using language.

He was just a fair faced adolescent
Whose zits were quite phosphorescent
He slapped on the cream
Wandered off in a dream
But the eruptions continued incessant.

No more a fair-faced adolescent
And zits slightly less phosphorescent
He's given up on the cream
Though he's still in a dream
Now his girlfriend is more acquiescent.

Years later this once adolescent
Thought fondly of zits phosphorescent
For his girlfriend has left
He's completely bereft
And his equipment is now obsolescent!

A. Autumn Term 1988 – Some of the things we did during the Poetry/Drama Carnival

19th Sept	ABC Theatre "Are there still Real Cowboys?"
	ABC Theatre Workshop
20th Sept	ABC Theatre Workshop
21st Sept	The Wilshers ("Words Alive")
9th Oct	Jui Dasgupta (Peripatetic harmonium teacher) and Win Shell (Teacher) read Tagore poetry in Bengali and English. Fourth year gave poetry morning to parents and toddlers.
10th Oct	Daylight Theatre "Shiver"
11th Oct	Mrs Cooter (Head–St Matthew's) read poetry.
15th Oct	Terry Waller (Librarian) read poetry. Parents–listened to third year poetry reading. John Burniston (Governor) read poetry.
16th Oct	Michael Langrish (Rector and Chair of Governors) read poetry. Fourth year gave poetry morning to parents and toddlers.
17th Oct	Miss Jackson (Head—Eastlands) read poetry. Pam Hulme (Teacher—St Andrew's Benn) read poetry.
18th Oct	Parents came to listen to first year poetry assembly. Parents joined in first year poetry lesson—listening.

(Timetable of events from St Andrew's C.E. Middle School, Rugby.)

Poetry, Drama and Music Carnival October 10th–21st at Studley High School

In the summer term, after the initial meeting with David Howe and a follow-up with Richard Watkins from Stratford High School to point us in the right direction, it was then up to us at SHS to organise a Poetry Festival. Clutching a list of likely poets, I sought advice from Mary Smith, my Head of Department. She recommended writer and lecturer Barrie Wade and so I tentatively telephoned him. Far from being uninterested or just too, too busy, he was delightfully accommodating. Somehow or other, we sketched out a possible timetable which I committed to paper, roughly allocating the local primary schools two sessions each with Barrie. He was to become known, most affectionately and respectfully, by the pupils as 'our local poet'.

Obtaining the Head's support for such a venture was not so simple. Not that he did not approve of such a scheme—far from it. He thought that the idea of a shared Poetry Festival between local schools an exciting venture, but, of course, the financial aspect posed a problem. Once he was assured that the West Midlands Art Council and Warwickshire County Council would pick up the bill for the hire of a poet, the Head's ideas began to really build up! Not only would we have a Poetry Carnival but we would involve music and drama as well! A Christian Theatre group 'Back to Back' and the Warwickshire Music Ensemble were already booked for October so why not incorporate those events, he suggested, and throw our doors open wide to the primary schools, invite them for sessions of drama and music (to be taken by Mrs Dot Tracey and Mr Roger Grainger) allowing the youngsters to share our excellent drama studio and music room? There was no holding Mr Parkes now!

By this time, the summer holidays were looming, so a meeting with the staff from the local schools was postponed until September. Despite the postal workers' strike we managed to meet and come up with an impressive list of events.

Firstly Barrie Wade spent two half-day sessions with each primary school and with us. These were excellent and greatly enjoyed and appreciated by everyone. Six primary schools visited us here at Studley for one hour of drama with Dot Tracey and one hour of music with Roger Grainger. The school caretaker, Dave Townson, donned his chauffeur's cap and chauffeured the little ones to and from our school. I'm not sure which proved more exciting to the children: the mini-bus ride had pride of place in their written work, but they responded magnificently to the sessions with Dot and Roger.

All this to-ing and fro-ing culminated in an evening for parents on Wednesday, 19th October here at SHS. How we managed to fetch all the lovely work from the primary schools and display it here seems like a miracle to me now—but we did, and our hall and entrance looked a wonderful sight, full of colourful and enthusiastic creativity.

We thought that the evening might last an hour but, due to the amazing work from all the schools, the evening grew and grew—it only ended two and a half hours later because the youngsters had to go home to bed!

Although somewhat chaotic, but never lacking in purpose, the evening was received with warmth by the parents and was a success. Somehow or other there were three hundred parents and children in our hall!

Thankyou, County, for setting us off along this track. We have all enjoyed it. Most of all we have enjoyed meeting each other. We might tackle this one again!

Joan Hughes

Bilton High School,
Rugby

Dear David,

I am sorry not to have written to you before this re. our Poetry Week. There are never enough hours in a day are there?

Overall the week was a happy time in which Poetry was definitely very prominent throughout the whole school. A great deal of activity involving a number of depts took place in the preceding weeks — competitious poetic tasks and display preparations. During Poetry Week displays/activities were to be seen/experienced in both our large entrance halls, the office, Special Needs, Maths, Computers, History, Typewriting, Cookery, Woodwork, Art, Pottery, Dance, P.E., Music, R.E., Biology, Rural Science depts and the Library (I may even have missed something out — oh yes, English!!) were all displaying poetry in various forms.

Some of the displays were superb. I was thrilled at the involvement of so many subject staff, and the enthusiasm of the children certainly developed as the week progressed.

Our assemblies each day were 'Poetry'. Each was compiled and performed by either junior (once), upper school (twice), or staff including caretakers (twice). These were very well received by pupils.

Competitions included:

a) poetry writing in a different topic for each year; (1) Celebrations, (2) School, (4) Memories, (5) Noise
b) limerick about Bilton High — open to all,
c) handwriting of a set piece of poetry — open to all, and
d) first to discover and name all poetry displays within school.

The final day was superb — Poetry Workshops in the morning, the visit of the Wilshers in the afternoon, the concert by Rugby Theatre and our pupil musicians in the evening.

There were a number of things I would have liked to have done if time had permitted, but it really was a hectic first half term, especially as normal classes, exam work, etc. had to be allowed to continue virtually uninterrupted.

Yours sincerely,

Joan Evans

Dear Mr Howe,

Please find enclosed a sample of the work done by children here during Kendell Smith's weekly sojourn.

The whole school found the time that Kendell spent with us a marvellous, positive experience. The staff always feel how much the success of any extended visit like this depends on the personality involved: Kendell soon dissipated any apprehensions! He had a quickly established rapport with all the classes, and developed good working relationships with all the age groups. This culminated in a series of class/group based presentations of written work plus an informal session of Kendell's own writings at the end of the week to which we invited parents and friends — this was controlled extremely well by Kendell, and he made it a priority to involve the children. Feedback from parents at this time, and at Parents' Open Evenings also held during that week, was very positive as apparently so many of the children had enthused about Kendell and his poetry.

The vast majority of children produced interesting work, some of it developed with accompanying music. It was all very new, and keenly received. Dub poetry now becomes another string to our bow, the influence of which we are sure will continue to grow. Already, when a choice of style was left open, several children attempted dub in their poetry drafts.

Kendell became part of our normal, flexible, everyday pattern — yet also special! This really does seem to have enabled his input to have been absorbed more deeply and long-lastingly — not just to be a 'one-off' event to be parcelled away. The children, with Kendell's help, chose the topics for their work, as we had decided against setting one particular theme.

We were fortunate that Mrs Chapman supplemented our computer equipment mid-week, although there was more copying out and re-drafting than initial writing as the children had mainly reached that stage. It did serve to whet our appetites further for this usage — if only we had more machines!

To sum up, the whole week was a great experience, well worth all the timetable juggling, red hot keyboard connections, *et al*!

Yours sincerely,

Sue Legge
Teacher i/c Language

B. Responses to the Residencies
Our Week with Amryl Johnson

I found out so much about poetry, speech, drama and people's feelings and ideas while Amryl Johnson was with us. I didn't realise how interesting and exciting walls could be, or how many ways there are to look at the theme we used. If I could look at everyday objects from so many different angles like Amryl did, I would feel as though I knew everything. All the talks we had in the English lessons were interesting and amusing. I enjoy reading poetry more now, because I can visualise the descriptions within the poems more vividly. I have also realised that one piece of writing can actually mean to you exactly what you want it to mean, and not just what the poet meant by it when it was written. Poetry is the best way of telling someone your feelings about something because it can be amusing, solemn, touching, sympathetic or romantic and, unlike a story, it is beautifully set out (usually) and lovely to read. So I believe that I learnt an awful lot while Amryl Johnson was in school and I think the whole week of poetry was very worthwhile.

(Pupil—Rugby High School)

Amryl Johnson's Visit to Knightlow Middle School

A great success. The theme for the afternoon was 'memories'. Amryl encouraged the children to think in terms of their senses and emotions. The thought patterns of many were captured by her poem 'Midnight' which is the story of the discovery of her cat in a London market.

Amryl then spent time explaining the story behind the poem and her use of words and phrases. She was able to show the children that economy of words combined with the correct flow or rhythm can create a successful piece of writing.

Before she arrived the children were informed a poet would be visiting the school for an afternoon to work with them. No other information was offered.

Their reaction was very uniform:

They expected a white male.
Someone elderly with grey hair.
Rather 'posh' and strict—severe almost.
They expected to have to write a lot.

They did not expect such a warm person who was so reassuring and friendly.

Their only criticism was they found her reaction to their responses rather patronising at times. Her favourite phrase was "That's wonderful". Obviously there were times when the children didn't agree that their answers merited such enthusiasm.

The children worked with Amryl for two hours and were given approximately another two to complete and re-draft.

Thankyou for making the event possible. It was successful, an occasion still referred to during lessons. A wonderful way to introduce poetry to children.

Yours,

Annette O'Leary

Short report on the "Amryl Johnson Week"

1. *My general and personal impressions*

I found Amryl Johnson to be a warm and pleasant personality. She was dynamic and charming with the students and certainly worked hard! (I thought, at our briefing meeting with her, that she was organising her meetings with our classes so as to be able to use material she was already familiar with, but I realised later that this was essential if she was to have any sort of structure for the week. Besides this, I can imagine that the work is different each time she meets a different group.)

2. *With Group IV*

Amryl explored fears and terrors with this group and held them spellbound for the first part of the session. For the second part they were writing.

One or two of the group lack powers of concentration to a desperate degree, but everyone tried her best according to her ability. At best, there was some very promising work produced, which the students worked over and handed in for Mrs Murphy to make a selection.

My students themselves were very enthusiastic when I asked them their views on Amryl and her session with them. They liked her personality and envied her ability to read poetry.

3. *With (Anon)*

This class had seemed the most unresponsive and suet-puddingy that I have ever taught, therefore I was not expecting too much here. Any results after a dreary start (not Amryl's fault, but theirs) were amazing, and still are having an effect on the class.

They have been doing interviews with elderly folk, and Amryl took this as a starting point for work on "memories". They couldn't get the hang of it at first, kept on putting their hands up and whining; and I think that even by the end of the second session, Amryl did not feel too happy about this group. Then about a week later the work started coming in until I had a fat sheaf of poems from every member of the class.

I found their insight amazing, and one of the poems so moving that I still find it difficult to read.

When I proposed making a tape they were delighted, and went into the 'auditioning' and selecting of poems with touching seriousness. They have now chosen the preferred list and are in the process of reading these onto tape—very nicely and clearly.

I should like Amryl to know just how successful this was, after an unpromising beginning—not just in terms of work produced, but in enthusing the class far beyond their normal inactivity.

A. P. Spiller

Report on visit of the Poet Amryl Johnson (With 2C and G. Forsythe)

At the planning meeting Amryl and Gillian Forsythe decided to take a theme: Amryl suggested 'Walls' but we also decided not to prime the girls.

Day 1 Monday 17th October, Period one. 2C were in their usual room, but we pushed back desks and made a circle of chairs.

Amryl pinned up a painting on the notice board which suggested several themes connected to 'Walls'. She then talked to the girls for about fifteen minutes on the many aspects of the theme and read us a poem of her own. She suggested links with personal growth; feelings of exclusion/inclusion, etc.

We then tried a spot of 'brain storming' but after a few ideas from individual girls like 'Berlin Wall', 'Great Wall of China' they fell rather silent — overawed by the occasion — so we broke into groups and discussion followed. Amryl and Gillian walked round listening and encouraging. Several impressive ideas emerged.

Day 2 Tuesday 18th October, Period one, usual room. A8 again. Stimulus picture still on the board but desks not moved today (G. Forsythe only). We started with a composite effort at creation. I explained what a dry stone wall was and drew a series of lumpy circles on the board slightly at random, with a pile of spare stones in a corner. I then asked for one word from each girl in turn and they automatically made the following poem — having to add one 'stone' only and it exactly fitted a class of 30 girls (which I had not planned!).

I like walls, High walls, low *walls* (added 'stone')
Any sort of wall at all.
Brown covered dumpy walls, climbing walls,
Grey stone, mossy, brick, wooden walls,
Sandy stone, ivy-creeping-over walls.

We liked this because we hadn't expected much from something put together by such strange arbitary means so that was a spur to greater things in small friendship groups.

Girls worked for the rest of the lesson on themes and some actually began to write first drafts.

Day 3 Wednesday 19th October, Period seven, Annexe One. (G. F. on own).

Gillian Forsythe went in with the Edward Lear pop-up box which the Post Office had produced. (On Monday's assembly Mrs Thornton had read the 'Pobble' poem.) I pointed out that English poets are rather fond of Nonsense and that some of their poems might be amusing on 'nonsense' lines. We then checked to see who knew any Lear and we all vaguely knew the 'Owl and the Pussy-Cat' so we recited it together, helping each other out when memories failed. This was an enjoyable corporate moment.

We then broke into groups again to carry on the work on poems begun on Day 2. Homework (officially on Monday, but not formally taken in this week) was also beginning to produce work which girls took along to show Amryl in the lunch hour.

Day 4 Thursday 20th October: Period seven, Hall.

This is our usual drama lesson so we began with a warm-up led by G. F. They all acted/reacted as individuals to a series of suggestions, e.g., 'You are trying to see over a wall which is almost as high as you can reach'; 'You climb to the top of a high wall and walk along it—dare you look down? Now try and get down again'; 'You are a young child and want to go downstairs to join your parents who are holding a party but you have been told to go to sleep'; 'You are in a cell, prisoner, it measures one meter by one by one', etc. Their mimes were very effective. We changed pace and emotion at least ten times. Then we broke into groups—largely the same as for Day 2 and 3 and this time it was suggested they made up a drama/mime on the theme but not (or not necessarily) involving a poem. Towards the end of the session these were presented to each other.

a) Social barriers. The down and outs in their soup kitchen: The yuppies in their chic restaurant. The former (in mime) physically broke through the wall and ousted the latter.

b) The maze. Chairs were placed to form a maze and a family outing with children and old grandma plus worried mother went to it—with some hiding and bumpings into each other—(light hearted).

c) Breaking in/breaking out. Using the stage and steps, burglars broke into a house but were caught in the act; tried to escape by climbing a wall. Later we saw them in prison and they tried to break out again. Well put together.

d) Breaking in/breaking out—again. One girl arrives at disco and the others exclude her from their group but then the outsider notices that the building is closing in upon them. Walls and ceiling crush down and the outsider is now included in the group as they all die in a tight heap. Didn't come over quite as powerfully because they didn't set the disco scene very obviously—since I *knew* what was going on it was more impressive to me than to the whole form (perhaps?).

e) Two girls played squash against an imaginary wall—very difficult to mime.

f) The last group was another breaking into a circle and we had no time to watch it.

Day 5 Friday 21st October. We had a double lesson in Annex 8, periods seven and eight (our usual lesson is P. 8 in An. 1). We pushed the chairs back again. Amryl was there and Mrs Collingham came to observe. We started by showing one or two of the dramatic pieces from the day before although some lost a little in the changed (cramped) surroundings. Then we returned to the poems which had been produced during the week and time was given to polish a presentation of these. Amryl and Gillian went round helping with finishing touches while individuals showed written poems to Mrs Collingham then we all presented:

a) Graffiti. A poem plus action—good social comment.

b) A very simple poem with a powerful punch line declaimed like a conversation between two people.

c) A descriptive poem recited by a group with some unison some single voice while the group sat in a wall formation and so on.

Disinterested comment could be gained from Mrs Collingham.

Follow up.

The next week was half term holiday and the week after that we simply had to prepare for 2C's first attempt at debating having had the debate moved from Monday to Friday in order to prepare. (Motion T.H.B. in ghosts.)

(2C all helped in the preparation and learnt quite a bit about effective argument and public speaking — they also incidentally gained the higher marks.)

Friday 4th November, P. 8. Having de-briefed on the debate I set as one of the homework choices a poem or piece of poetic prose on the Wall theme and asked for all other writings to be handed in by the next week and canvassed opinion on video recording selected dramas and readings of poems in our Thursday drama lesson. Decision — Yes.

Personal comment: I found the excercise most stimulating/enjoyable. Amryl did spark off ideas but I was chiefly impressed by what the girls (and even myself) managed after her initial input.

Her presence in school and for assembly was warmly welcomed and the whole week felt cohesive and well planned for 2C since we started and ended with Amryl there and ended with so many polished performances although the creative writing could still continue.

G. Forsythe.

P.S. One of the homework choices was to write an evaluation of the poetry week.

P.P.S. The poetry now received includes some of very high quality in my opinion.

Active Learning, English and I.C.S.S.

The following report was written by children involved in an English lesson which was supported by two members of the intercultural Support Service—a body which promotes intercultural understanding in schools.

Children had discussed several aspects of the theme "Outsiders" which constituted an exploration of the thoughts and feelings of "minority" groups, e.g., tramps, the disabled, etc. The aim of the exercise was to encourage children to explore their own thoughts and feelings about other people and to try to identify the reasons for which people might be classed as "outsiders".

The I.C.S.S. activity involved the children in the creation of two very different community groups. It was tremendous fun but, more importantly, the children came to a fuller understanding of the need for communication between different "cultures" and in the final discussion it was clear that the exercise had been a success.

S. Pether, Head of English
(Etone School)

Kendell Smith's Visit to Our School

On the 2nd November a young, lively, humorous and friendly poet called Kendell Smith came to Etone, our school. This poet made me laugh a lot but his poems were a mix of humour and serious talk. The thing I liked best about him was he was nothing like a teacher. He talked to you as free as you like, which made me able to speak all my thoughts as well. His poetry was unlike the usual poems you read in books. His poetry really comes alive. I liked his poetry because he sings it to music, sort of like a rap. He called this technique, Dub Poetry. He joked a lot, but he could talk about serious things really well. Another thing I liked about his poems was he made them mean a lot. They had a lot of feeling in them. This helped me to understand how to write a better poem, how to make it rhyme and make sense in what I write to make it mean something.

He talked about many things in this world, that could be made better. I made up a poem set on those terms. I liked Kendell in himself very much.

Report by Clare Mason

Discussion of Visit of Oscar Frank

T	Do you think that having Oscar in school will have changed people's attitudes?
Geoffrey	Yes
Robert	Yes
Bobby	Yes
T	How and why? I mean how will it have changed? Scott?
Scott	Because most people will stop being racialist now.
T	But why?
Scott	Because they've seen how nice they are.
Geoffrey	They've got to know — they've got to know other people.
Robert	They won't call them names or anything now.
T	So they've got to know a grown-up who's a black person.
Robert	They're just like English people — like a black person is just like an English person.

★★★

T	How did you feel about writing your own poetry? What was it like when you were first sent off to do that? Davinder?
Davinder	I thought it would be hard because — um — you don't know the rhythm and you're not professional but then when I'd finished the poem I though "Oh, that was good".
Robert	It was all right for me because I started something and Oscar Frank goes up to me and he just starts helping me and he puts — he puts down a few words for me.
Scott	Miss — the only thing I didn't like about it was having to write it out.
Robert	He said — "You can write that yourself now".
Davinder	He was a great help.
Scott	Miss — he didn't come into our class.
T	He didn't come in to one class, did he. Kelly?
Kelly	When I first started a poem it was quite hard because I didn't know what to put and then when I'd got started a bit more it got easier. I put down some words — crossed out the ones I didn't want.
T	Have you learned any new techniques for writing poetry?
Scott	Yes.

Robert	Yes.
Davinder	Yes.
T	What have you learned about approaches to writing poetry?
Nicol	Um—I've learned that—um—it sounds better if you put—if you put—um—sort of—like—chorus then a verse and then a sort of chorus again.
T	Yes, because you did that with your poem, didn't you?
Davinder	Like in the poem he read.
T	Like in "The Banana Man".
Rupinder	I've learned—like, put a word down that you're gonna need in the poem and see what rhymes with it, and then make up things.
Scott	That's what I thought as well, Miss.
T	Anybody else learned any other approaches to writing poetry?
Scott	Yes—with him here I felt that I could write better—poetry and that.
T	Why did you feel that, Scott—with him here? What difference does it make having him here?
Scott	Because of the great help he made—because he's a professional he can help you write poems.
T	All right, so he gives you the confidence, does he, to write poems?
All	Yes.

C. Poetry Workshops in Warwickshire Schools

Report

Introduction

During November and early December 1988 I have led a series of nine Poetry Workshops in various Warwickshire schools. The age-range of children attending has been from four to ten years of age.

Process

The workshops took the form of an exploration of the 'creators' in our society, e.g., poets, artists, musicians, followed by a 'listening to words' session, which included word association games and, with the younger ones, a look at Nursery Rhymes and how words match the action. In every case I read a number of poems to the children throughout each session and helped the children to write their own joint poem on a topic I had introduced, e.g., Christmas, sailing on a ship (a ship in a bottle being used to encourage their imagination), animals, etc.

Conclusion

All the sessions were very enjoyable and the children took an enthusiastic part. There were in each school a number of children (perhaps 4–20) who had obvious imaginative word skills and it was very fascinating to me to see how quickly these children could be identified. All the children however became excited at the link between words and emotion and I was impressed by their participation and the work they produced both in classroom and subsequent to my visits.

Averil Redman
December 1988

D. Words Alive!

On the 19th of October it was the third day of my school's book week. In this, we have lots of different activities and on Wednesday we had a visit from Jill and Barry Wilsher.

They came to talk about poetry. Jill and Barry were very good at telling poems. The first thing that they did in the morning was to warm their voices up. They did this by making shapes with their jaw then sang a few notes.

Their first poem was "Switch on the Night". They used their voices to the full. It was really exciting. In the middle of a poem they would stop for a period of time and they kept you in suspense until they started again.

There were eight poems in all and I enjoyed every one of them. There was one poem that nearly had me in tears. This was called "The Death of a Cat". It was written by a boy aged between sixteen and seventeen. It was all about a cat that had been ill for four days and on the fifth day it died. It described everything perfectly. I had an enjoyable morning.

Jodyne Smith
19th October

Bishops Tachbrook School

Dear Sarah,

We thoroughly enjoyed the visit of Jill and Barry Wilsher and their selection of poems.

We are focusing on poetry for the whole year and are having our 'Poetry Week' in the summer. I think the visit has really inspired us all!

Many thanks,

Ronda Ramsay (Mrs)

Timetable — WORDS ALIVE

Monday 10th

A.M.

Nathaniel Newton First
Victoria End
Chapel End
Nuneaton

Contact:
Debbie Hibberd

Tel. Chapel End 392236

Three performances

Start 9.15 am (1) 5/6 yrs (2) 6/8 yrs (3) 6/7 yrs

P.M.

Atherstone North Middle
Carlyon Road
(off Ratcliffe Road)
Atherstone

Contact:
June Maiden

Three performances

1.00 pm (1) 8/9 yrs (2) 9/10 yrs (3) 11/12 yrs

E. List of Schools whose Work is Represented in the Anthology

Alcester Infants
Aylesford Comprehensive, Warwick
Atherstone North Middle
Brookhurst C.E. Combined, Leamington
Baddesley Ensor First
Bilton High
Bishops Tachbrook C.E. Combined
Cashmore Middle, Leamington
Coten End Middle, Warwick
Coughton C.E. Junior and Infant
Our Lady and St Teresa's R.C. Combined, Cubbington
Cubbington C.E. Combined
Curdworth C.E. First
Dunchurch C.E. First
Etone Comprehensive, Nuneaton
Gaydon Junior and Infant
Henley Junior and Infant
Hillmorton Paddox Middle
Knightlow C.E. First, Stretton on Dunsmore
Knightlow C.E. Middle, Stretton on Dunsmore
Long Lawford Combined
Michael Drayton Middle, Hartshill
Newbold C.E. Junior and Infant
Park Hill Middle, Kenilworth
Polesworth Nethersole's C.E. Middle
Priors Field Combined
Queen's C.E. Middle, Nuneaton
Rokeby First, Rugby
Rokeby Middle, Rugby
Rugby High
St Andrew's C.E. Middle, Rugby
St Anthony's R.C. Combined, Leamington
St John's First, Kenilworth
St Paul's C.E. Combined, Leamington
St Mary's R.C. Junior and Infant, Studley
St Thomas More, Nuneaton
Stockingford First
Stockingford Middle
Stratford High
Studley C.E. Junior
Studley High
Tanworth in Arden C.E. Junior and Infant
Telford Middle, Leamington
Tredington C.E. Junior and Infant